D1505714

SURVIVING NATURAL DISASTERS

ELITE FORCES SURVIVAL GUIDE SERIES

SURVIVING NATURAL DISASTERS

PATRICK WILSON

**Introduction by Colonel John T. Carney. Jr., USAF—Ret.
President, Special Operations Warrior Foundation**

MASON CREST PUBLISHERS

This edition first published in 2003
by Mason Crest Publishers Inc.
370 Reed Road, Broomall, PA, 19008

Library of Congress Cataloging-in-Publication Data available

ISBN 1-59084-016-X

Editorial and design by
Amber Books Ltd.
Bradley's Close
74–77 White Lion Street
London N1 9PF

Project Editor Chris Stone
Designer Simon Thompson
Picture Research Lisa Wren

Printed and bound in Malaysia

10 9 8 7 6 5 4 3 2 1

ACKNOWLEDGMENT

For authenticating this book, the Publishers would like to thank the Public Affairs Offices of the U.S. Special Operations Command, MacDill AFB, FL.; Army Special Operations Command, Fort Bragg, N.C.; Navy Special Warfare Command, Coronado, CA.; and the Air Force Special Operations Command, Hurlbert Field, FL.

IMPORTANT NOTICE

The survival techniques and information described in this publication are for use in dire circumstances where the safety of the individual is at risk. Accordingly, the publisher cannot accept any responsibility for any prosecution or proceedings brought or instituted against any person or body as a result of the uses or misuses of the techniques and information within.

DEDICATION

This book is dedicated to those who perished in the terrorist attacks of September 11, 2001, and to the Special Forces soldiers who continually serve to defend freedom.

CONTENTS

INTRODUCTION

Elite forces are the tip of Freedom's spear. These small, special units are universally the first to engage, whether on reconnaissance missions into denied territory for larger, conventional forces or in direct action, surgical operations, preemptive strikes, retaliatory action, and hostage rescues. They lead the way in today's war on terrorism, the war on drugs, the war on transnational unrest, and in humanitarian operations as well as nation building. When large scale warfare erupts, they offer theater commanders a wide variety of unique, unconventional options.

Most such units are regionally oriented, acclimated to the culture and conversant in the languages of the areas where they operate. Since they deploy to those areas regularly, often for combined training exercises with indigenous forces, these elite units also serve as peacetime "global scouts" and "diplomacy multipliers," a beacon of hope for the democratic aspirations of oppressed peoples all over the globe.

Elite forces are truly "quiet professionals": their actions speak louder than words. They are self-motivated, self-confident, versatile, seasoned, mature individuals who rely on teamwork more than daring-do. Unfortunately, theirs is dangerous work. Since "Desert One"—the 1980 attempt to rescue hostages from the U.S. embassy in Tehran, for instance—American special operations forces have suffered casualties in real world operations at close to fifteen times the rate of U.S. conventional forces. By the very nature of the challenges which face special operations forces, training for these elite units has proven even more hazardous.

Thus it's with special pride that I join you in saluting the brave men and women who volunteer to serve in and support these magnificent units and who face such difficult challenges ahead.

Colonel John T. Carney, Jr., USAF–Ret.
President, Special Operations Warrior Foundation

Elite troops are provided with training to cope with natural disasters. Here, soldiers look for survivors following an earthquake in Taiwan.

EARTHQUAKES, LANDSLIDES, VOLCANOES, AND AVALANCHES

Simply being aware is one of the keys for coping with natural disasters. Elite soldiers are always alert, watching for both the potential dangers of the region and the correct course of action to take.

Earthquakes

Earthquakes are impossible to predict, and can have a number of different classifications—**tectonic**, volcanic, and artificially produced. No place on Earth is free from the danger of an earthquake. Most earthquakes occur at the edges of tectonic plates. Plates either slide against each other, or one under the other, but there are plenty of examples of earthquakes that do not occur at the edges of plates.

The danger of an earthquake is usually its effect on man-made structures or the triggering of such things as landslides and tidal waves (**tsunamis**).

Recording an earthquake

The **Richter Scale** is a means of measuring the strength of an earthquake. It was introduced in 1935, and named after Charles Frances Richter, who invented it. It is based on a rating system of 1–10, 1 being a very insignificant earth tremor, 10 a huge quake of

Lava generally flows slowly but, with a heavy emission and a steep slope, it can reach speeds of 14 miles per hour (22 km/h).

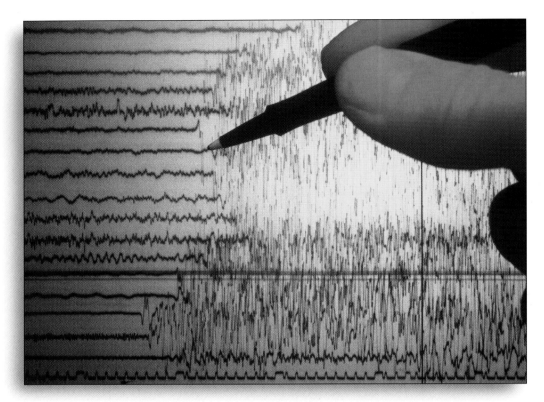

A seismograph showing earthquake activity. A seismograph is an instrument that measures the force and direction of earthquakes.

catastrophic proportions. There has never been a quake that has registered more than 9 on the scale.

Force of earthquake	Scale
Not felt but recorded on **seismometer**	2.6
Widely felt	3.5
Local damage	4.5
Destructive earthquake	6.0
Major earthquake	7.0
Great earthquake	8.0+

The Mercalli Scale

This scale is another method of testing earthquake strength, named after Giuseppe Mercalli, the Italian geologist who invented it. The grading is as follows.

I.   Felt by almost no one.

II.   Felt by very few people.

III.   Tremor noticed but not recognized as an earthquake.

IV.   Felt indoors by many.

V.   Felt by almost everyone. Trees and poles swaying.

VI.   Felt by everyone. Furniture moved.
        Slight damage.

VII.   Everyone runs outdoors. Considerable damage to poorly
        built structures.

VIII.   Earthquake-resistant structures damaged.
        Others collapse.

IX.   All buildings considerably damaged.
        Cracks in ground.

X.   Many structures destroyed. Ground badly cracked.

XI.   Almost all structures fall. Bridges wrecked. Wide cracks in
        the ground.

XII.   Total destruction. Waves seen on ground.

Ground

Earthquake effects can be worse on soft ground, which tends to amplify the shockwaves, particularly mud and clay soils. This also applies to waterlogged, low-lying regions. Steep slopes can be dangerous because of the risk of landslides.

Preparation

A soldier will put together essential supplies such as water, canned food, a battery-powered radio, and a flashlight.

Action

The action required to safely survive an earthquake will vary depending on where the soldier sits out the tremors.

Sheltering indoors is the most common. If a soldier is inside a building, he or she will get under a strong table or some other protection, and hold on during the tremors. If soldiers cannot get underneath something, they will get close to an inside wall. Soldiers are trained to always keep away from heavy objects like book cases. They do not attempt to run out of a building during an earthquake,

Some earthquakes have the power to be massively destructive. Roads can be torn apart (as shown here) and buildings can be flattened.

since they will be at great risk from falling and flying objects. Finally, they keep away from any glass, such as windows or mirrors, that might shatter.

The other situation in which elite soldiers are most likely to find themselves is stranded outdoors. There are several rules soldiers follow to avoid being injured or killed. They do not try to run away from the earthquake, because they are likely to find themselves running into danger. They keep away from trees, buildings, or other structures that might fall on them. They keep clear of telephone poles, electric towers, and wires. They will never try to touch or move an electric cable that has fallen.

Finally, soldiers may find themselves on the road, driving a car or army vehicle, when disaster strikes. If this occurs, soldiers should slow down and drive to a clear place, away from underpasses, lampposts, or trees. They will then stay in the car until the shaking stops.

Volcanoes

Volcanoes are formed by the outpouring of lava and other fragment material. There are a number of active volcanoes around the world as well as some volcanoes, such as Mount Vesuvius (in Italy, outside Naples), which are dormant.

Dangers

When a volcano erupts, lava mixed with steam and other gases is forced out of the earth and forms a thick cloud. The lava rises inside the vent of the volcano, some pieces shoot up into the air, and more lava flows over the crater. Some lava may emerge from a secondary vent in the side of the volcano.

The lava flow is generally slow moving, although this is not always the case. **Pahoehoe** is a smooth lava that forms a ropy surface. **Aa** is sharp and twisted, and tends to flow faster than pahoehoe. The latter flows at about three feet (1 m) per minute, though if the slope is steep and the lava flow is heavy, this speed can increase to 14 miles per hour (400 m per minute). Aa tends to move in surges, piling up each time before moving on.

As well as lava, the volcano can throw out material that ranges from fine ash to eight-ton bombs that can travel up to three miles. This flying material, or **pyroclastic flow**, is the most dangerous element of the volcano, since the lava itself, with a certain amount of warning, can be avoided without too much difficulty.

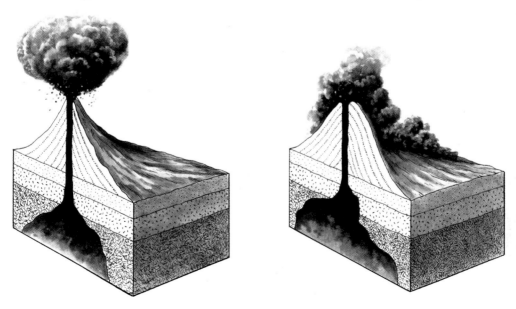

Two types of volcanoes—vulcanian (on the left) and pelean (on the right). Both can cause severe damage.

A sight that is equally beautiful and terrifying. The power of molten lava is such that it destroys anything in its path.

Aa flow, such as this in Hawaii, tends to move quickly and in surges. Once it has cooled down, however, lava solidifies into rock.

Another highly destructive characteristic of some volcanoes is **nuees ardentes**, or glowing clouds. These are ground-hugging clouds of molten lava fragments, which can move with great speed down a mountain.

Secondary effects

Secondary effects from a volcano include earthquakes (normally before the eruption), flash floods, landslides and mudflows, thunderstorms, and tsunamis.

In Colombia, in 1985, a volcano led to a landslide of mud and rock that buried a whole town and its inhabitants. Since the soil on the edges of volcanoes is fertile, larger numbers of people than ever before are willing to take the risk of living in a high-risk area. Therefore the presence of people in an area does not mean it is safe.

Prediction

It is difficult to accurately predict a volcanic eruption, just as it is difficult to predict an earthquake. One of the best indications of timing is to look at the pattern of past eruptions of a volcano. An earthquake always comes before an eruption, though the time can vary from hours to months.

Preparation

Troops always stay aware of the warning systems in their area. They remember that some countries have better warning systems than others, so they are always prepared to make their own judgments about danger signs when necessary. If in doubt, they are trained to always be cautious, since even highly experienced volcanologists have been killed by volcanoes.

They make sure they have an evacuation plan prepared. Ideally, this should involve getting to high ground as far away from the eruption as possible. They also prepare an alternative route.

Action

- Elite soldiers will equip themselves with goggles and some kind of breathing mask. If they do not have a mask, they will hold a damp cloth over their faces to help them breathe.
- They will avoid low-lying areas if possible because of the danger from flash floods.

- They do not cross a low-lying area or go over a bridge when a mudflow is approaching. Mudflows can move at two miles (3 km) an hour.

Aftermath

- Troops must beware of inhaling ash—they keep a mask on or use a damp cloth.
- They keep goggles on.
- They are careful of the danger of heavy ash, which can cause a roof to collapse.

U.S. soldiers at an evacuation center in the Philippines, set up to house some of the 83,000 homeless civilians after a volcanic eruption.

Landslide and mudflow

Prediction

There is usually little or no warning of a landslide or mudflow, but the following signs can be an indication to soldiers. Inside a house, doors stick; cracks appear in plaster, tiles, and bricks. Outside, cracks begin to appear in the ground and sidewalk; water comes out of

The force of this mudslide in Italy in September 2000 buried a parked car.

the ground in places where it is not normally found; fences and trees move; and there is a rumbling sound.

Action

Soldiers must be prepared for landslides or mudflows to strike at any time, so it is essential to know what action to take.

If they are inside, soldiers will shelter under a sturdy object, such as a table, and hold on until the threat passed. If they happen to be outside at the time of the disaster, soldiers must get out of the path of the landslide or mudflow as quickly as possible (remembering that they cannot outrun it). They will then head for the nearest high ground, which is out of the direct path of danger. If they are caught, they must curl up in balls and protect their heads.

Avalanches

An avalanche, the fall of mass quantities of snow at great speed, can occur wherever large amounts of snow lie, but it is influenced by certain conditions. If the snow is well bound together, then the risk of an avalanche is reduced. If there are marked differences in the hardness of layers of snow, then the risk of an avalanche fall increases.

Elite soldiers can assess the likelihood of an avalanche by digging into the snow in a possible danger area to test the hardness. If they prod the snow with an axe shaft and notice sudden changes in resistance, that is quite a good sign that the area is likely to have avalanches. They can perform the test more thoroughly by digging a snow profile, preferably all the way to the ground, which will let them assess differences in hardness, moisture content, and crystal size in the various layers of snow.

Dangers

If the snow is very wet, it will be more likely to slide. A rough guide to the wetness of snow is that if soldiers can make a snowball out of the snow, it is very wet. If their gloves are dripping wet from handling the snow, it is extremely wet. If the slope is **concave**, it is less likely to have an avalanche. If it is **convex**, it is more likely to have an avalanche. Obviously, the angle of the slope is also an important factor. The steeper the slope, the more likely the snow is to slide off of it. Slopes of between 20 degrees and 50 degrees are most likely to have an avalanche.

The most common type of avalanche is called "wind slab," and is caused by the effect of wind on falling or fallen snow. Wind slab snow is chalky in appearance, has a fine texture, and makes a squeaky noise when walked on.

Avalanches can also be caused when powdery snow builds up in conditions of no or little wind. Over 16 inches (40 cm) of fresh snow is an indicator of a high risk of this kind of avalanche.

Avalanches caused by ice usually occur in warm weather when ice masses fall after thawing. Pinnacles of ice are most likely to fall in the morning or evening, due to the change in temperature.

A rapid rise in temperature or an area exposed to direct sunlight makes the risk of a wet snow avalanche greater. A soldier should see if there are snowballs running down a hill, which is an indicator of this kind of avalanche.

The awesome sight of an avalanche in the Swiss Alps in 1999. Few people have any chance of surviving an avalanche of this size.

During the course of their operations, the British Special Air Service (SAS) can often find themselves in difficult situations in the snow. They are given instructions on what to do in areas of avalanche.

- Soldiers should cross a danger zone one at a time, connected by a rope.
- Soldiers should cross the slope as high as possible.
- They should take advantage of any available protection, such as rock outcrops.
- If soldiers are caught in an avalanche, they should do their best to maintain their present position. This may mean digging with

Elite troops are often called in to help in the aftermath of natural disasters. Here, an army rescue helicopter comes to the aid of victims of an avalanche in Colorado.

an axe into an area of snow above them that is not moving. By staying where they are, they will let the dangerous snow pass safely below them.

- If soldiers are falling in an avalanche, they must try to move across to the side of the fall by rolling sideways. They should use swimming motions to try to remain near the surface. If they are still caught in the avalanche when it has stopped, they must use all their energy to "swim" to the surface.
- If they are buried, they should try to clear a breathing space in front of the ice.
- They should conserve oxygen by not shouting, which is unlikely to be heard anyway.

Rescue procedures

If soldiers see someone taken by an avalanche, they must mark the spot where they saw the person before the avalanche fell, and then the place where the avalanche hit the person. They then follow the line through these two points, and continue it below to find the most likely place of burial. They are trained to call for help but not to move from the area to find assistance if it is more than 15 minutes away. They then try to look for anything like personal items that may indicate where the burial site is. They must regularly check the area by probing with an axe shaft or other means.

On finding the victim, they will clear the mouth and airways. It is important to remove the weight of snow from the chest. If the person is not breathing, **artificial resuscitation** is immediately given, even before removing the body from the snow.

FREAK WEATHER CONDITIONS

To ensure they are not caught unaware by freak weather conditions, elite soldiers keep in touch with meteorological (weather) warnings. This may involve carrying a battery-powered radio. They will make sure that they have emergency supplies on hand, just in case.

Hurricanes

A hurricane is a storm with winds of between 74 and 200 miles per hour (120 and 320 km/h). Hurricanes have their source in equatorial waters, particularly the Caribbean Sea and the Gulf of Mexico. In the western Pacific Ocean they are known as typhoons, and in the Indian Ocean and around Australia they are known as tropical cyclones.

Dangers

The destructive power of a hurricane can be displayed in different ways, including wind power, tornadoes, rainfall, and storm surges. The storm surge is the most dangerous aspect of the hurricane, accounting for 90 percent of deaths. It is caused by changes in atmospheric pressure inside the hurricane sucking up the sea. Hurricane winds also pile up the water against the coastlines. The resulting wall of water can be up to 40 feet (12 m) high, though it **diminishes** as it heads inland.

A satellite image of Hurricane Floyd, which hit the coast of Florida in 1999. Elite troops were immediately called in to provide help.

High winds, as seen clearly in this picture of palm trees, provide an early indicator of an oncoming hurricane.

Forecast

It is difficult to forecast a hurricane. Even **meteorological** offices in developed countries can be caught with their guard down, with devastating consequences.

Hurricanes tend to be more common in the Atlantic region in August and September. The source of the hurricane consists of warm water influenced by the Earth's rotation. The sea temperature must be at least 79°F (26°C). Hurricanes occur at least four to five degrees poleward from the equator, but no closer.

When there is a threat of a hurricane occurring within the next 24 to 36 hours, a Hurricane Watch is issued. If a hurricane is expected in less than 24 hours, a Hurricane Warning is issued. During a hurricane, troops must just watch, listen to a battery-powered radio for updates, and make preparations.

The **Saffir-Simpson scale** of storm intensity is commonly used to measure the effects of hurricane-force storm.

Storm category	Wind speed mph (km/h)
Tropical storm	31–73 (50–116)
Hurricane	
Level 1 (Weak)	74–95 (118–152)
Level 2 (Moderate)	96–110 (153–176)
Level 3 (Strong)	111–130 (177–208)
Level 4 (Very strong)	131–155 (209–248)
Level 5 (Devastating)	156 + (249 +)

This diagram shows how a hurricane forms. Warm air spirals upward in the center (eye); air sinks into the eye from above.

Boarding windows and securing properties is the first stage in preparing for a hurricane, as shown by these civilians in Miami in 1999.

Preparation

- Soldiers will first board up windows in a building.
- They are well aware that taping up windows will not help.
- They will trim any weak branches off trees that are near houses.
- They must also bring inside any objects, such as garbage cans or garden chairs, that the wind could pick up.

Action

If a hurricane strikes while elite troops are indoors they will shelter in the cellar or somewhere away from windows or the roof. In some cases, a hurricane can rip the roof off of a house. Soldiers do not drop their guard when the calm eye of the storm passes over. The other side of the storm, with winds traveling in the opposite direction, will soon reach them.

If troops are outside when a hurricane approaches, they must find cover as soon as possible. A cave, ditch, or rocky outcrop in which to shelter is best. Troops must always be prepared to adjust their position when the eye of the storm has passed over. Under no circumstances do they attempt to drive a car in a hurricane. Finally, they avoid bridges, which may be damaged or washed away.

Tornadoes

Tornadoes are much more unpredictable than hurricanes. The track of a tornado is erratic, and so all the more dangerous. A tornado will not give much time to plan and think. Elite troops know they have to be ready to act fast.

A tornado looks like a gray spiral, funnel, or elephant's trunk, and wind speeds can be anything from 300 to 350 miles per hour (480–560 km/h). It is made visible by the dust that is sucked up by the winds and by condensed water droplets. The area of the tornado touching the ground is usually only a few hundred feet (tens of meters) across, though it can be half a mile (1 km) at its widest point.

A tornado can tear a house apart by creating higher pressure inside the house than outside.

FUJITA-PEARSON TORNADO SCALE

F–0: 40–72 mph (64–115 km/h)	Chimney damage, tree branches broken
F–1: 73–112 mph (116–179 km/h)	Mobile homes overturned
F–2: 113–157 mph (180–251 km/h)	Considerable damage, mobile homes demolished, trees uprooted
F–3: 158–205 mph (252–328 km/h)	Roofs and walls torn down, cars and trains overturned
F–4: 206–260 mph (329–416 km/h)	Well-constructed walls leveled
F–5: 261–318 mph (417–509 km/h)	Houses lifted off foundations, and carried great distances; cars thrown as far as 330 feet (110 m)

Preparation

The usual course of action taken by troops is to first find a cellar or tornado shelter before the storm arrives. They remember that, even if the tornado does not appear to be heading in their direction, it may suddenly change course.

A tornado photographed in northeast Denver in 1988. As it is hard to predict the direction of tornadoes; they can hit areas unexpectedly.

Action

In order to survive the threat of tornadoes, elite troops must be prepared to take evasive action if they are inside a building, or outside, when the wind strikes.

If inside, soldiers will shelter in the basement or lowest level of the building. They take cover in the center of the room, away from corners and windows. They shelter under strong furniture, such as a heavy table, and hold onto it. They protect their heads and necks with their arms.

A soldier rescues a child from floods in Venezuela. Following any natural disaster, the rescue of children is the army's first priority.

If they are outside, elite soldiers will not walk around because they know they could be plucked up by the wind or be struck by heavy objects thrown by the wind. They do not stay in a car but get out and find the most solid shelter available. They will shelter in a ditch if necessary or under a sturdy rocky outcrop.

Lightning

Lightning is a visible electrical discharge between clouds, or between a cloud and the Earth. More people are killed by lightning than by any other natural **phenomenon**. But it is easier to protect yourself from lightning than from an earthquake or a hurricane.

Prediction

Although there is such a thing as a bolt from the blue (lightning out of a clear, blue sky), the most likely source of lightning is from dark thunderclouds. If troops see them approaching, they take precautions immediately.

Lightning is accompanied by thunder. Since light travels faster than sound, elite soldiers can estimate the distance in miles between themselves and a thunderstorm by counting the seconds that elapse between the lightning and the thunder, and then dividing by five. They are still in danger from lightning, even if the storm is far away.

Protection

An elite soldier can try and protect a building from lightning by attaching a metallic rod, wired to the ground, to the highest part of the roof.

Forked lightning has a high electrical charge, which means troops must not touch any electrical appliances during a thunderstorm.

Action

To be caught indoors during a thunderstorm is much the better place to be, but it is far from safe and soldiers must still be careful. They will always stay away from telephones, electrical appliances, computers, and in particular, televisions because of the electricity charge generated by lightning. They will not use faucets in sinks or bathtubs because metal pipes and water conduct electricity.

If outside, elite soldiers remove any metal objects they are wearing. They will not shelter under a single tree, because the lightning is likely to strike the tree. Instead, they lie flat on the ground if they are exposed in a thunderstorm. If possible, they will find a ditch or depression to lie in. If they feel their hair standing on end out in the open, they will bend forward and put their hands on their knees. They will adopt a low crouching position with their feet together and hands on ears to minimize thunder shock.

If they need to take shelter in a cave, they make sure they go as deep inside as possible. They do not stay near the mouth of the cave. In addition, they will avoid water, high ground, and open spaces.

Floods

Floods are a common and very dangerous form of natural disaster, especially for those parts of the Earth's population (approximately 60 percent) that live beside coasts, river **deltas**, and **estuaries**.

After rainfall, water is absorbed by the soil and vegetation, or by evaporation. The remainder, called the **runoff**, runs into streams and rivers. When the runoff is too large, and streams and rivers cannot contain it, a flood is caused. Intense rainfall over a small area causes flash floods.

Preparation

Elite troops always find out about water levels and floods in the place to which they are traveling. They are also trained to fill bathtubs, sinks, and buckets with clean water, in case the water supply becomes **contaminated**. They keep in touch with flood warnings on a battery-operated radio.

The aftermath of a typhoon that hit Hong Kong in 1998. Flash floods are a regular by-product of these storm-force winds.

Action

If soldiers are inside a building during a flash flood, they will collect vital supplies, and move to an upper part of the house. Elite troops will be prepared, if necessary, to climb out onto the roof. Of course, they will also take warm clothing. They take some rope with them to tie themselves and others to a stable structure, such as a chimney stack if they are on the roof.

• If soldiers are outside, they will make their way to high ground. They do not, if at all possible, wade through flood water. If they are in a vehicle that has stalled, they must abandon it and get to high ground as quickly as possible.

A U.S. Army soldier helps civilians through flood waters following the destruction caused by Hurricane Floyd in 1999.

THE SEA

Around 71 percent of the Earth's surface is covered by water. It is therefore vital that troops learn how to survive in this environment. Humanity's natural domain is land, and that makes survival at sea for any length of time a massive challenge. The dangers posed by the sea should not be underestimated.

The sea is pitiless when it comes to survival situations; the first mistake you make in a maritime emergency is likely to be your last. Elite soldiers must master every ocean survival technique in order to live in this unforgiving environment.

Waterspouts (the marine equivalent of tornadoes) are particularly common off the Atlantic and Gulf Coasts of the United States, and along the coasts of China and Japan. Hurricanes and typhoons occur in the warm areas of all oceans during the summer and fall. They can last for up to two weeks. Capsizes, shipwrecks, and a whole host of problems can happen.

Elite soldiers must know what to do if they find themselves in the water. Their first action when they hit the water should be to make their way to a raft. If none is available, they must try, if possible, to cling to a large piece of floating debris. Throughout this time, they will try to stay calm: a relaxed body will stay afloat. Elite soldiers are trained to float on their backs; this requires less energy than

A remarkable picture of an ocean waterspout, a phenomenon particularly common off the Atlantic and Gulf Coasts, taken in 1943.

WHEN ABANDONING SHIP

Abandoning ship is a frightening experience, but you must act quickly. Elite troops follow these SAS guidelines to save themselves.

- Elite soldiers will put on warm, preferably woolen, clothing, including hat and gloves. They will also wrap a towel around their necks.
- They will take a flashlight.
- They will grab chocolates and hard candies if possible.
- They do not inflate life jackets until they leave the ship.
- When jumping overboard, they will first throw in something that floats and jump close to it.

Air trapped in clothing will help buoyancy: they make sure they do not take off their clothes in the water.

swimming facedown. Alternatively, they will float facedown on the surface with their arms outstretched and legs pointing toward the bottom. To breathe, they raise their heads and place their arms in an outstretched position again.

Soldiers must try to conserve their strength when they are in the water. They use a variety of these swimming strokes when they have survived a disaster.

Storm waves break over an army vessel in the Arctic Ocean. The sea is unpredictable and must be treated with respect at all times.

A dummy pilot is rescued by an accident and emergency team during a training exercise. The U.S. Navy SEALs are experienced at sea rescue.

- Dog paddle: good for when an elite soldier is clothed or wearing a life jacket.
- Breast stroke: good for swimming underwater or in rough seas.
- Side stroke: a useful relief stroke because only one arm is needed to maintain momentum and buoyancy.
- Back stroke: another good relief stroke. It relieves the muscles that are used for other strokes.

Cold water

If the water is cold, soldiers risk dying of **hypothermia**. They must get into a raft and insulate their bodies from the cold bottom of the raft.

If there is no raft, they should keep still and assume the Heat Escape Lessening Posture (**HELP**), because this will increase survival time. Around 50 percent of the body's heat is lost from the head. Therefore, they must try to keep their heads out of the water.

If there are several soldiers in the water, they will huddle close in a circle to preserve body heat. But these measures are only temporary—soldiers know they must get out of the water.

Picking up survivors

If soldiers are in a life raft and are rescuing people in the water, they will try to throw a line with a life belt attached. Alternatively, they will send a swimmer out with a line attached to a flotation device. They will approach the person from behind to avoid getting kicked,

A Sea-Air rescue crewman being expertly lifted into the safety of a helicopter during a training exercise in March 2000.

grabbed, or scratched. It is important to grab the survivor by the back of the life jacket or take hold under the chin, and then use a sidestroke to drag the person to the raft. The soldier should try to reassure the person. Troops are trained not to underestimate the strength of a person in a state of panic in the water.

Movement

Soldiers must remember one thing when afloat in the ocean: their rafts will be at the mercy of winds and currents. Currents flow in a clockwise direction in the northern hemisphere, and counter-

clockwise in the southern hemisphere. Sea currents travel at speeds of less than five miles per hour (8 km/hr), so movement is going to be very slow. In areas where warm and cold currents meet, there will often be storms, dense fog, high winds, and heavy seas. These will make movement difficult and dangerous.

Winds and waves can aid raft travel. Winds blow in an easterly direction in tropical areas, the so-called trade winds, and from the west in regions at higher **latitudes**. To

By adopting the HELP position, keeping her head above water, the survivor can increase her survival time in cold water.

take advantage of the wind, soldiers need a sail. If the raft does not have one, they should make one using a poncho or other piece of material.

To move or stay put?

If an SOS has been sent or if soldiers know they are in regular shipping lanes, they should stay in the same location for up to 72 hours. However, if they are off the shipping lanes and have not been able to send a signal, then they should get underway as soon as possible to take advantage of their fitness and **stamina**. Their first action is to head in the direction of land. If there is no land nearby, they will try to work out where the nearest shipping lane is and head in that direction.

Signaling

If they have them, troops first use flares and dye markers (which spread brightly colored dye in the sea) to attract the attention of a ship or aircraft. If they do not have any signaling equipment, then they must attract attention by waving clothing and other materials, brightly colored if possible. Dye markers should only be used in daylight. (They normally last for around three hours.)

All flares should be handled carefully. They must be kept dry and secure. When they are fired, they are pointed upward and away from anyone else in the raft. They must be used only when it is likely that the soldier will be seen.

A shiny, reflective surface is also an excellent way of attracting attention and can be used for long-range signaling.

If elite soldiers have a radio transmitter in their life raft, it will have preset frequencies at 121.5 and 243 megahertz, and will have a range of around 20 miles (32 km). The soldiers should try to transmit at frequent intervals, but they must be careful not to run down the batteries. (If they have a watch, they will use it to time signals at regular intervals, remembering to keep the watch dry).

Getting ashore

Once soldiers have sighted land, their primary goal is to reach it as safely and quickly as possible.

If they are swimming, they should wear their shoes and at least one thickness of clothing. Side or breast stroke is the best way to

U.S. Navy SEALs are trained to cope in any circumstances at sea. Having a raft will always increase their chances of survival.

conserve strength. Water is calmer in an area of heavy growth of seaweed. Troops do not swim through it; they crawl over the top by grasping the vegetation.

If soldiers are in a raft, they must choose their destination point carefully. They will not land when the sun is low and straight in front of them, and they will avoid coral reefs and rocky cliffs. Similarly, they will stay well clear of **rip currents** (strong surface currents) or strong tidal currents. Soldiers should use oars and paddles if they have them, and they will adjust the sea anchor to keep a strain on the anchor line. This will prevent the sea from throwing the stern around and will keep the raft pointed toward the shore.

In heavy surf, soldiers try to avoid meeting a large wave at the precise moment it breaks. As they near the beach, they will try to ride the raft on the crest of a wave. They will not jump out until the raft has grounded, and will then get out quickly and pull it ashore.

Indicators that land is nearby

As a survivor at sea, your number-one priority is to reach land. Keep a lookout for the following objects and signs that can point to land.

- Clouds. Cumulus clouds (fluffy, white ones) in a clear sky are likely to have been formed over land. In tropical areas, a green tint on the underside of clouds is caused by the reflection of sunlight from the shallow water over coral reefs.
- Birds usually fly from land before midday and return to it in the late afternoon. Beware of lone birds, though: they may just be disorientated.

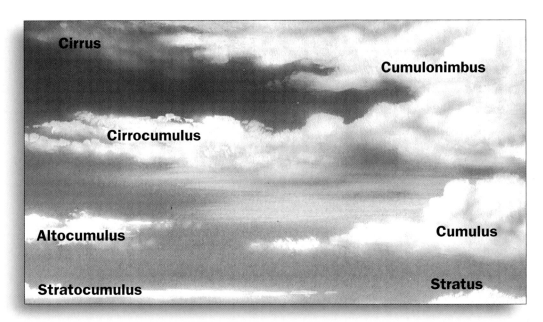

This diagram shows the range of different types of cloud in the sky. If you can see cumulus clouds, it is likely that land is not that far off.

- Coconuts, driftwood, and drifting vegetation can sometimes indicate that land is near.
- A change in the direction of sea movement may be caused by the tide around an island.
- Water that is muddy with silt has probably come from the mouth of a large river that is nearby.
- Deep water is dark green or dark blue; a lighter color indicates shallow water and perhaps land.

Swimming ashore

When elite soldiers are in the water and approaching a shoreline, they are still in potential danger. These are the tactics adopted by the U.S. Navy SEALs to land safely:

- Ride in on the back of a small wave by swimming forward with it.
- In high waves, swim toward the shore in the trough between waves. Face and submerge beneath waves, then swim forward in the next trough.
- If caught in the undertow of a large wave, let it pass over and then push off the bottom with your feet or swim to the surface if in deep water.
- When landing on a rocky shore, aim for the place where the waves rush up onto the rocks, not where they explode with a high white spray.
- To land, advance behind a large wave into the breakers. Face the shore with your feet in front, two to three feet (60–90 cm) lower than your head. In this way, your feet will absorb shocks when you land or hit submerged rocks or reefs, and you will not get injured.

Fully armed Navy SEALs coming ashore. They are experts at swimming ashore even when heavily laden with equipment.

If you do not reach shore behind the wave you have selected, swim using your hands only. Adopt a sitting position as the next wave approaches, and it will carry you to shore.

Dangers

The many dangers at sea, such as hostile fish, the threat of starvation and thirst, and the cold and wet, can all be dealt with to varying degrees, though troops are trained to always remember that they will rarely get a second chance at sea. They must stay alert!

Antishark measures if you are in the water

SEAL team members are often on operations in shark-infested waters. They have tried and tested antishark measures. Their instructions to training troops are:

- If you are in a group in the water, bunch together and form a tight circle for added protection.
- Face outward and keep a lookout for sharks.
- Ward off an attack by kicking a shark. Only use your hands as a last resort. Use a hard object, such as a knife, and aim for the snout, **gills**, or eyes.
- Because sharks will be attracted by the scent, urinate in short, sharp bursts, and let it dissipate between spurts. Collect feces and throw as far away from you as possible. Try to reswallow vomit or, failing that, throw it as far away as possible.
- Stay as quiet as possible and float to save energy.
- If you have to swim, use strong regular strokes, not frantic

irregular movements. (These will make sharks believe you are a wounded fish.)

- Do not swim directly away from a shark; instead, face it, and swim to one side, using strong, rhythmic movements.

Medical problems

In a raft, elite soldiers will not expose themselves to the sun and wind needlessly. They will keep layers of clothing on at all times, especially on their heads. Any injured persons should be placed on the floor of the raft and be made comfortable. They must be kept warm or cool, depending on the climate they are in, and as dry as possible. Sunglasses or eye shields will be worn, if available, to protect the eyes from the sun's glare. Elite soldiers should be extra careful about reflection off the water, which intensifies the sun's rays. They are also aware that prolonged exposure to saltwater may produce cold sores. Troops should therefore keep their clothing as dry as possible. Sores should be cleaned and **antiseptic cream** applied. Large sores must be covered with a dressing, and the dressings changed regularly.

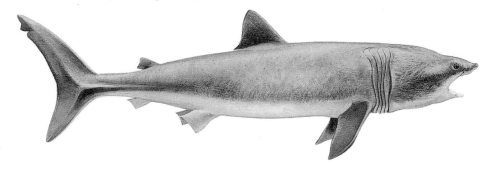

The basking shark (above) is harmless to humans. The species of shark that do attack people include the great white and the hammerhead.

Water

The lack of drinking water is a major problem for survivors at sea. Whatever water they have must be rationed at once. Troops should never relax the ration: they do not know how long they will need it. Troops never drink seawater or urine.

Water is a precious for military pilots who are stranded behind enemy lines. The following are the Canadian Air Force guidelines for reducing your body's overall use and loss of fluids:

- If you do not have any water, do not eat.
- In hot climates, reduce loss of body fluids through perspiration by remaining inactive.
- Brush dried salt off of the body with a dry cloth.
- Try to sleep and rest as much as possible to minimize fluid loss.
- Try not to get seasick. Vomiting means losing valuable fluids. Relax and focus your mind on other tasks.
- Do not drink alcohol; it dehydrates the body.
- Do not smoke; it increases thirst.

Tsunamis

Tidal waves called tsunamis are caused by earthquakes. It is difficult to predict a tsunami from the behavior of waves at sea, since tsunami waves might travel a long way at a height of no more than three feet (1 m), and therefore pass by ships unnoticed. When they reach land, however, they can be about 50 feet (15 m) high. Japan's worst tsunami produced a wave 80 feet (24 m) high.

Tsunami alerts are issued on the basis of earthquake reports. Although this system can work well for places that are far enough

WATER RATIONS

At sea, fresh water is your most precious commodity. Follow these water ration rules to increase your chances of survival:

Day 1. Give no water: the body can make use of its own water reserves. Be strict with this rule.

Days 2–4. Give 14 fluid ounces (400 ml) if available.

Day 5 onward. Give 2–8 fluid ounces (55–225 ml) daily, depending on water availability and climate.

away from the earthquake, it is often the case that the tsunami will have struck before the warning can be given.

Elite troops should keep in touch with earthquake warnings at all times and beware any unusual rumblings.

Preparation

Elite troops must plan an escape route to an inland location that is above the likely height of any approaching wave. They will put together an emergency kit with food and first aid.

Action

- They do not head toward the beach to check if they can see a wave approaching. If they can see it, it is too late to escape.
- They are trained to remember that a series of waves may be involved, so they must not return to the danger area until there is a complete all-clear.

DROUGHTS AND FIRE

Soldiers must be alert to the dangers of drought and fire during their missions. Drought is most common to Africa and other areas of very low rainfall; fire can occur in any dry climate.

Drought

The average person needs just under a pint of water each day to stay alive. In the United States, **drought** is defined as less than one-tenth inch (2.5 mm) of rainfall in 48 hours. In Britain, an absolute drought is defined as a period of 15 days with less than one-hundredth inch (0.25 mm) of rain each day. In India, a drought is declared if the rainfall is less than 75 percent of the average.

Major droughts tend to occur at latitudes of about 15 to 20 degrees, in areas that border on the permanently dry areas of the world. Africa is more at the mercy of droughts than any other area. Seasonal rainfall in Africa can show large variations within the season, and tends to fall in short and intense storms. The rain can also be very localized.

Preparation

Troops need to have a store of water, and need to take care that water supplies do not become contaminated during a drought. They make sure that all water is boiled before drinking.

A wildfire rages in Wancrest Park, near Pine, Colorado, in June 2000. Wildfires can generate winds of up to 75 miles (120 km) per hour.

A drought-dry riverbed in Somalia, North Africa. To survive such hostile conditions without water requires excellent survival training and luck.

Fire

Dry land and drought can lead to bush fires. Australia is especially prone to these, with the native eucalyptus tree being a prime culprit in the spread of fire. There tends to be a great deal of dry bark and other matter on the floor of Australian forests, providing good fuel for fires. The amount of litter, and the time that has elapsed since the last fire, are critical in judging how intensely a fire will burn.

Types of fire

Ground fire: Burns below the surface of the Earth in layers of organic material such as peat. It tends to smolder, having no flame and little smoke. It is difficult to control.

Surface fire: Includes grass fires and forest fires that burn debris on the forest floor. It can also burn the lower branches of trees.

Crown fire: Burns the tops of trees and is dangerously unpredictable. It can burn ahead of the surface fire.

Spot fire: Caused by burning leaves and bark being blown ahead of the main fire, causing secondary fires elsewhere, sometimes many miles away.

Prevention

- Troops take great care when lighting a camp fire, especially in a dry area.
- They use a constructed fireplace or light the fire in a trench at least one foot (30 cm) deep.
- They take care that tree roots do not catch fire.
- They clear the ground in the area at least 10 feet (3 m) from the camp fire.
- They do not light a fire when conditions are hot and windy, and when the bush is very dry.

If elite soldiers see a fire starting, they will use a branch with green leaves to damp it down or use any available fire-fighting equipment. They do not swing the flames around because this will spread the fire. They must also remember that fires burn more rapidly uphill, and that burned material can roll down the hill.

Action

If they are trapped by a fire, elite soldiers must try to:
- Crouch in a pond, lake, or river.
- Look for shelter in a clear area or among rocks.

- Lie flat, and cover their bodies and heads with wet clothing or with some soil.
- Breathe the air close to the ground to avoid scorching their lungs or inhaling smoke.
- As a last resort, if they see an opening, and the fire is not too deep or too high, they can attempt to dash through the flames to the area behind them that has already been burned. They will need to be absolutely resolved to go all the way through and not try to turn back. If the flames are higher than head height, they will not attempt to run through them.
- If they decide to dash through the flames, they must cover as much of the surface of his body as possible, and dampen clothes and hair if they have water.
- If their clothes catch fire, they will not stay on their feet once out of the fire, but will crouch down.
- Soldiers do not try to escape a fire by running uphill, unless absolutely necessary.

Beware of accidents

Troops must be aware that there may be a multitude of accidents waiting to happen after any of the emergencies listed in these chapters have occurred. They need to watch out for the following:

- Fallen power lines, which could electrocute them if they touched them. There may be damage to electrical systems within buildings.
- **Ruptured** gas mains.
- Fires and floods.
- Dangerous flammable or toxic fluids and materials.

- Broken water pipes and contaminated water.
- Burst sewage pipes.
- Aftershocks that can bring down weakened structures.
- Animals, even tame ones, becoming more dangerous. They treat all animals with caution.

Elite troops need to use common sense and caution at all times.

With very little rain and tinder-dry leaves, Australia has a major problem with bush fires. In these conditions, spot fires are common.

GLOSSARY

Aa Sharp and twisted volcano lava that flows quickly.

Antiseptic cream Cream to prevent infection.

Artificial resuscitation Helping a patient to start breathing again by blowing in the mouth and pushing on the chest.

Concave Hollow-shaped.

Contaminated Containing harmful substances.

Convex Bulging outward.

Delta Triangle-shaped area containing the mouth of a river.

Diminishes Reduces.

Drought Period of very low or no rainfall.

Estuaries Where rivers meet the sea.

Gills Breathing organ of a fish.

HELP (Heat Escape Lessening Posture) Position used to increase survival time in cold water.

Hypothermia Extremely cold and dangerously low body temperature.

Latitudes Imaginary parallel lines north and south of the Equator.

Meteorological Weather. Meteorology is the study of weather patterns.

Nuees ardentes Ground-hugging clouds of molten lava fragments.

Pahoehoe A smooth, slow-moving lava that forms a ropy surface.

Phenomenon A peculiar or extraordinary happening or event.

Pyroclastic flow Flying material from a volcano.

Richter Scale The means of measuring the size of earthquakes.

Rip currents Surface water currents.

Runoff Rainfall water, which runs into streams and rivers.

Ruptured Broken or strained.

Saffir-Simpson Scale Used to measure the wind speeds of hurricanes.

Seismometer Instrument for measuring earthquakes.

Stamina The physical strength to keep going under pressure.

Tectonic A branch of geology concerned with the study of the Earth's crust.

Tsunamis Another name for tidal waves.

EQUIPMENT REQUIREMENTS

Clothing and shelter
Thermal underwear
Thin layer of synthetic material
Woolen or wool mixture shirt
Woven fiber sweater or jacket (normally a fleece)
Waterproof and windproof final layer
Two pairs of socks (minimum)
Compact, light, windproof pants with numerous pockets with zippers,
    to carry items securely
Waterproof pants
Gloves—leather or mittens
Balaclava (a tight woolen garment covering the head and neck)
Spare clothing—socks, underwear, shirts, etc.
Soft, well-maintained leather boots
H-frame bergen (backpack) with side pockets
Portable, lightweight, waterproof shelter
Matches

Survival tin
A knife
Matches
Flint
Sewing kit
Water purification tablets
Compass
Mirror
Safety pins
Wire
Plastic bag
Antiseptic cream
Snare wire

Survival bag
Pliers with wire cutter
Dental floss (for sewing)
Folding knife
Ring saw
Snow shovel
Signal cloth
Fishing hooks and flies
Weights and line
Multivitamins
Protein tablets
Large chocolate bar
Dried eggs
Dried milk
File

Cutlery set
Three space blankets
Four candles
Microlite flashlight
Extra battery and bulb
Fire starter
Windproof and waterproof matches
Butane lighter
Insect repellent
Snares
Plastic cup
Slingshot and ammunition
Knife sharpener
Whistle
Soap
Two orange smoke signals
Mess tin

EQUIPMENT FOR HOSTILE TERRAINS

Desert
Light-colored clothing (reflects sunlight)

Cloth neckpiece
Sunglasses or goggles

Tropical regions
Talcum powder
Insect repellent
Machete
Hammock
Mosquito netting
Tropical medicines

Polar regions
Waterproof and windproof outer layers
Many inner layers of clothing for insulation
Goggles
Three layers of socks
Waterproof canvas boots
Ice axe
Ski stick
Rope

USEFUL WEBSITES

http://www.fema.gov
http://www.disasternews.net
http://www.disaster.net
http://www.pbs.org/wnet/savageearth
http://www.spc.noaa.gov
http://members.tripod.com/dogw
http://quake.wr.usgs.gov

FURTHER READING

Borofka, Michael. *Emergency Survival Guide—You Can Survive Anything.*
   Carmel, Calif.: Ventana Gear, 1994.
DaCosta, Tenaj and Wiseman, George. *Do-It-Yourself Crisis Survival.*
   Columbus, Ohio: Eagle Research, 1999.
Darman, Peter. *The Survival Handbook.* Mechanisburg, Pa.: Stackpole
   Books, 1996.
Department of Defense. *US Survival Manual.* New York: Apple Pie
   Publishers, 1992.
Junchaya, Kellye A. *They Laughed at Noah: Preparing for Natural Disasters.*
   Colorado Springs, Colo.: Medcap, 1999.
Piven, Joshua and Borgenicht, David. *The Worst Case Scenario Survival
   Handbook.* San Francisco, Calif.: Chronicle Books, 2001.
Roskind, Robert A. *The Complete Disaster Home Preparation Guide.*
   Des Moines, Ia.: Prentice Hall, 2000.
Van Tilburg, Christopher. *Emergency Survival: A Pocket Guide.*
   Seattle, Wash.: Mountaineers Books, 2001

ABOUT THE AUTHOR

Patrick Wilson was educated at Marlborough College, Wiltshire and
studied history at Manchester University. He was a member of the Officer
Training Corps, and for the past seven years he has been heavily involved in
training young people in the art of survival on Combined Cadet Force
(CCF) and Duke of Edinburgh Courses. He has taught history at St.
Edward's School, Oxford, Millfield School, and currently at Bradfield
College in England.

His main passion is military history. His first book was *Dunkirk—From
Disaster to Deliverance* (Pen & Sword, 2000). Since then he has written *The
War Behind the Wire* (Pen & Sword, 2000), which accompanied a television
documentary on prisoners of war. He recently edited the diaries of an
Australian teenager in the First World War.

INDEX

References in italics refer to illustrations